CONTENTS

CHOICE

Karen McCarthy Woolf • *Unsafe* • Bloomsbury

RECOMMENDATIONS

Joe Carrick-Varty • *Before Violence* • Carcanet Press
Wayne Holloway-Smith • *RABBITBOX* • Scribner Editions
Keith Jarrett • *Hide Me Under the Blood and I Shall Be Satisfied*
Bad Betty Press
Jennifer Wong • *Light Year* • Nine Arches Press

SPECIAL COMMENDATION

Rita Ann Higgins • *Jiving with Wasps* •*New and Selected Poems*
Bloodaxe Books

TRANSLATION CHOICE

Chen Yuhong • 不可能的天堂 • *Impossible Paradise* • *Selected Poems*
Translated by George O'Connell and Diana Shi • Carcanet Press

PAMPHLET CHOICE

Fatema Abdoolcarim • *Tremble* • Monitor Books

Poetry Book Society

Poetry Book Society Memberships

Choice

4 Books a Year: 4 Choice books & 4 *Bulletins* (UK £65, Europe £85, ROW £120)

World Poetry

8 Books: 4 Choices, 4 Translation books & 4 *Bulletins* (£98, £160, £190)

Complete

24 Books: 4 Choices, 16 Recommendations, 4 Translations & 4 *Bulletins* (£230, £290, £360

Single copies of the *Bulletin* £12.99

Cover Artwork: *The Time of Mom and NANA* by Fumi Yanagimoto @fumiyanagimoto

ISBN 9781913129873 ISSN 0551-1690

Supported using public funding by ARTS COUNCIL ENGLAND

MIX Paper | Supporting responsible forestry FSC® C014866

Poetry Book Society | Milburn House | Dean Street | Newcastle upon Tyne | NE1 1LF

0191 230 8100 | enquiries@poetrybooksociety.co.uk

WWW.POETRYBOOKS.CO.UK

LETTER FROM THE PBS

Happy New Year and welcome to our first poetry magazine of 2026. Entering the 10th year of our stewardship of the Poetry Book Society feels like a reason to celebrate. It's also a time to reflect and thank *you*, our wonderful community, who have supported us throughout this journey. We know times are tough but every membership, donation and book sale continues to have a huge impact – thank you!

A big thank you to our out-going 2025 Selectors Yomi Ṣode, who has championed new poetries with such energy and enthusiasm, and Shivanee Ramlochan who opened up the Translation Choice to the truly global. We're delighted to welcome Fred D'Aguiar and Leo Boix to our team of Selectors. Fred D'Aguiar is an award-winning British-Guyanese poet, US based Professor and Newcastle Poetry Festival supporter. Argentine-born Leo Boix is a Forward Prize shortlisted poet, translator, editor and advocate for Queer and Latin American poetry. Each brings exciting new perspectives from the transatlantic to the Latinx to our selections.

The Spring Selections capture the current moment, both the difficult and the beautiful, and shake us out of everyday complacency. *Unsafe* by Karen McCarthy Woolf examines race, class and what it means to be a citizen in the US and UK today. Keith Jarrett interrogates police violence and Queer Black identity. Joe Carrick-Varty charts the after-shocks of trauma in formal schisms and Wayne Holloway-Smith leads us into a "rabbitbox" of domestic threat, where a mother and child storytell their way out of fear. The Irish "people's poet" Rita Ann Higgins lends humour and heart to everyday lives and the Translation Choice Chen Yuhong urges us to appreciate each "flowering moment". While Jennifer Wong reflects on migration, motherhood and an apt state of "always beginning", as we enter this new year.

Spring is, indeed, a chance to begin afresh, read deeply and see the world anew, so there's no better time to reconnect with our poetry community. On the 17th February we hosted our in-person Spring Showcase with Karen McCarthy Woolf and Jennifer Wong at Newcastle University with NCLA. If you missed it, you can still join our free Online Spring Showcase (details in Member's Area) on the 9th March to hear readings by Karen McCarthy Woolf, Joe Carrick-Varty and Keith Jarrett, hosted by Victoria Kennefick. Alternatively, tune into Arji's PBS Podcast (www.poetrybooks.co.uk/pages/the-pbs-podcast) for interviews about the craft behind the Choice or visit the Members Area to access digital discussion notes.

We hope these Spring Selections resonate deeply with you, bring solace or spark inspiration, as you start your year of poetry discovery.

ALICE KATE MULLEN, PBS MANAGER

MEET THE SELECTORS

BOOKS

Victoria Kennefick: “Another season and another reason to celebrate a fragrant new bouquet of brilliant poetry collections coming into bloom. How lucky we are! This quarter’s offerings are very special indeed, the perfect accompaniments to the lightening evenings and an essential resistance to the shadows that continue to try to drag us away from our true essence. How grateful I am for these poems and how they defend against the darkness, while never doubting its existence.”

Fred D’Aguiar: “It’s official, the isle really is full of noises, and from overseas too, which makes the PBS Spring Selections a cornucopia, a reliquary, a harbinger (some good, some urgent, all solidly crafted) for any reader, and, it must be said, a juicy challenge for the PBS Selectors.”

TRANSLATION

Leo Boix: “Each poem in *Impossible Paradise* 不可能的天堂 opened a door I hadn’t expected. Yuhong’s curiosity is contagious, her generosity unstoppable. Guided by translations of rare tact and imagination, I found myself travelling further with every page, until choosing it no longer felt like a judgement but like an instinctive choice.”

PAMPHLETS

Yousif M. Qasmiyeh: “Poetry is seen with a third eye. I read my fellow poets’ submissions while thinking of the state of the world, of our shrinking planetary, and yet from what I have seen and read, I catch hope, a sense of recreation, and the desire to retell what we have, and do not have, with fresher eyes. The pamphlets I hold in my hands have rendered the words and the world visible and textural, for all to see and feel.”

MEET OUR REVIEWERS

DAVE COATES is a critic and essayist based in Edinburgh. He was a co-organiser of the Ledbury Critics Programme, and his writing has appeared in *Poetry Review, Poetry London, The Stinging Fly, Extra Teeth, catflap, spamzine* and many other magazines. He has been a reviewer for the PBS *Bulletin* since 2021.

JENNY DANES is a poet and facilitator whose work has appeared in *Poetry Wales, The Rialto, Magma, Under the Radar, Basket*, and *bath magg*. In 2016 she won The Poetry Business' New Poets Prize, and her pamphlet *Gaps* was published by Smith|Doorstop. Find out more at www.jennydanes.co.uk.

BETH DAVIES is the current Sheffield Poet Laureate 2024-26. Her debut pamphlet *The Pretence of Understanding* was published by The Poetry Business after winning the 2022 New Poets Prize. Find out more at www.bethdaviespoet.wordpress.com.

JASMINE GRAY is a Northern writer published in *Anthropocene, The London Magazine*, and *The Double Negative*. She has published two Broken Sleep pamphlets *Let's Photograph Girls Enjoying Life* (2019) and *Open Your Mouth* (2023).

KAYLEIGH JAYSHREE is a poet and a Roundhouse Collective alumna who has performed her poems at Glastonbury Festival. Her pamphlet *Mango and Starblush* was published by fourteen poems.

GREGORY KEARNS is a writer based in Liverpool. He has been published in *Bath Magg, The Mersey Review* and *Not About Now*. He has worked with English Heritage and No Dice Collective and hosts The Poems We Made Along The Way podcast.

ROSE SCHIERIG is a poet and MA Writing Poetry student at Newcastle University. She graduated with a BA in English Literature with Creative Writing from Newcastle University in 2024. You can read her writing @fromrosamund on Instagram.

SHASH TREVETT is a poet and translator of Tamil poetry into English. Her collection *The Naming of Names* was published by Smith|Doorstop (2024). She is a Ledbury Critic and a Trustee of *Modern Poetry in Translation*. She has been a reviewer for the PBS *Bulletin* since 2021.

Image: Fiona Melville

KAREN McCARTHY WOOLF

Born in London to English and Jamaican parents, Karen McCarthy Woolf is the author of two poetry collections and editor of seven literary anthologies. Her novel-in-verse *Top Doll* was shortlisted for the T.S. Eliot Prize and the Jhalak Prize for Poetry. She was poet in residence at the Promise Institute for Human Rights as a postdoctoral Fulbright Scholar at UCLA. In 2025, she won a Society of Authors Cholmondeley Award and the Jerwood Prize for Poetry (England).

UNSAFE

BLOOMSBURY | £12.99 | PBS PRICE £9.75

Unsafe by Karen McCarthy Woolf is a profound interrogation of territory and access and how individuals, groups and spaces are patrolled, controlled and contained. The title itself is suggestive of the traumatic outcome of dysfunctional, enforced, unequal, and violent boundaries – a lack of safety. McCarthy Woolf skilfully measures and records the reverberations of colonialism across London and LA charting the effects of capitalism on those who live at its unforgiving edges:

Of lawns landscaped to rust, liverish
as dogs' piss in summer's drought, windswept.

The epigraph from John Clare's 'The Village Minstrel' an autobiographical poem that combines various poetic genres, foreshadows McCarthy Woolf's project. As the politics of enclosure face a belated reckoning, *Unsafe* is an absorbing reflection on place, the body, nature, and the self. Just as Clare uses the churchyard to symbolise how the enclosure movement and the resultant social changes distort the lives and deaths of the villagers, McCarthy Woolf uses the blighted urban landscape to investigate how this transformation leads to alienation and worse.

Our demise a triptych
on the walls of multi-storey, glassy cathedrals:

McCarthy Woolf combines several genres weaving together poetry, visual documentary, and lyric essay. The black and white photograph that opens the collection depicts a shattered windowpane still replete with its wire mesh. The cracks through the glass reach out in all directions like the visual representation of a scream. The landscape is post-industrial, a post-apocalyptic wasteland – all lines and angles – but with its own brutal beauty as the sun, its light still clear in monochrome, touches the foreground of the picture rendering it disturbingly and conversely perfect – "epic as it was causal".

Unsafe grapples with the pain of feeling displaced and whether it's via tattoos, blackberries, "A pilfered blackberry / is a sin", or the emblematic essence of cats, McCarthy Woolf curates and collects evidence of the impact of gentrification and class division. Like Clare, the poet here powerfully observes her own history from the outside, interrogating what it means to be a citizen and composing a moving and urgent hymn in praise of our few remaining third places.

VICTORIA KENNEFICK

KAREN McCARTHY WOOLF

In 2019 I moved to LA as a Fulbright Scholar at UCLA's Promise Institute for Human Rights. I'd been to California many times. I love the nature: the desert, ocean and canyons are stunning, but living in the city was different. The tech boom had spiked housing costs and iconic spots like Venice Beach were full of tented encampments, often occupied by priced-out locals. The sharp, if familiar, contrast between America's lavishly housed and the unhoused had never felt so stark. LA's like that: on Friday I'd be at a meeting of grassroots activists opposing carceral algorithms in Skid Row, while on Saturday I'd be in a Hollywood mansion reading poems at a fundraiser attended by Elon Musk's mum.

Having grown up in London, I'd been writing about place and gentrification, and thinking about how race and class intersect with climate and nature for a while; sometimes using the *Zuihitsu*, which incorporates the quotidian in its synthesis of multiple narrative threads. Layli Long Soldier's *Whereas* and John Clare's poems and journals were also on my desk; *Unsafe* is bookended by a disrupted *glosa* (a medieval Spanish intertextual form) responding to his work on the enclosures.

My postdoc was cut short by the pandemic, and I returned to lockdown in the UK. Three of my siblings died. We witnessed the killing of George Floyd. Suddenly the more abstract aspects of my research into precarity and the body under settler capitalism felt concrete. Throughout the period I'd been taking photos as an aide-mémoire, for socials and as a visual component of my practice, where the phone is an extension of the body. Now it feels like these images are part of a new digital language that shapes the lexicon and here, the overall composition, so the borders between one long poem and photo lyric blur.

KAREN RECOMMENDS

When I first read '38' in Layli Long Soldier's *Whereas* (Picador, 2019) it moved me in a way that only poetry can. It was profoundly transformative and I was able to connect what I had experienced through my body as I stood on the high plains of South Dakota at Pine Ridge, the ancestral land of the Lakota people, to a laser-precise interrogation of language, metaphor, history and geopolitics. It will always be one of my favourite books, and I recommend it to anyone who wants to understand America.

EXTRACT

At a time when gentrification was intensifying in London, and elsewhere around the world—

At a time when state violence against Black, Brown and working-class people continues to intensify, I started to think tattoos were a new territorial act—

I started to think a tattoo was a way to reclaim agency over the body as our access to and freedoms within public space diminished.

EXTRACT

Tents deemed to have marred
the view are removed:
residents gunned down
when they protest   against hostile fire.

With many a loss to them the truth is known.

JOE CARRICK-VARTY

Joe Carrick-Varty is a British-Irish poet, writer and founding editor of *bath magg*. He is the author of two pamphlets: *Somewhere Far* (The Poetry Business, 2019) and *54 Questions for the Man Who Sold a Shotgun to My Father* (Out-Spoken Press, 2020). His work has appeared in the *New Statesman, The Poetry Review* and *Poetry London*. He won an Eric Gregory Award in 2022. His debut *More Sky* was shortlisted for the Michael Murphy Memorial Poetry Prize 2025 and the T.S. Eliot Prize 2023.

BEFORE VIOLENCE

CARCANET PRESS | £12.99 | PBS PRICE £9.75

Joe Carrick-Varty's remarkable debut *More Sky* charted the action of trauma on our perception of time, reality, love, and identity. *Before Violence* delves further into the long-term repercussions in poems that are utterly original, devastating, and compelling. Divided into three sections, the poems weave in and out of time from the "violent / picnics" of youth through to "What happens when you tell a secret?" to the final elegiac section lamenting the heartbreaking loss of a much-loved friend:

> the relief on Sunday at the festival
> when word of a security guard seeing you
> reached our circle of tents your tent
> as you left it quiet as a cathedral will you forgive
> me when i say i got drunk that night

And forgiveness, in all its forms, is at the heart of this collection replete with a wide variety of poetic forms from the shattered lyric to diary-like prose poems. This intention is signposted from the very beginning on the dedication page simply inscribed, "for us". This gift to "us" is an indication of the generosity of perception, spirit, and attention Carrick-Varty brings to the subjects and language of each poem. In particular, he writes about his sister very empathetically and lovingly in poems like '90s, Baby' and 'People Die When You're Not Looking' about their shared, yet unique, experience of trauma:

> ...sister tell me
> how old is the oldest child   in your body
> how young is the last star   of its sleep

This continues in the second section which interrogates the very nature of writing poetry and its inherent risks – not to mention the invisibility of process and the skill and care required to "tell it like it is", but also preserve the integrity of subjects and the privacy of the events. Carrick-Varty confronts the possible intention of the poem, the form, the theme – and the poet – with characteristic and confrontingly invigorating self-awareness, "Autobiographical writing as vehicle for sympathy. Where the author, the protagonist, is rendered the hero of their own tragic story". Death, loss, and the anxiety of legacy stalk this book – but from those shadows the possibility of healing also emerges – most memorably in the form of a new kitten, "at times the kitten felt like a child i had lost". This is an exceptional collection from one of the UK's most exciting contemporary poets.

VICTORIA KENNEFICK

JOE CARRICK-VARTY

The pair of words "before violence" had been kicking around in my head for a few years before I started writing this book. Sometime towards the end of 2020, when I was finishing my first book *More Sky*, I was thinking a lot about family, about love, and about violence, asking: where does my experience fall within this three-pointed star?

Violence carried out within a family, domestic violence if you will, often happens in tandem with love – at least that's my experience – which makes for a confusing and complicated lens through which to examine childhood.

It is my belief that the violence I experienced as a child – the violence that has echoed throughout my teens and into my adult life – was echoing long before I was born. My father once described it as a kind of weather, snow that's been falling and falling, "fields and fields of white".

But cycles of violence carried out across generations leave little room for a future without suffering. So what then? I think this book is my attempt to answer the questions I have been asking myself all these years: How can love and violence coexist within a family? Where does the violence come from? Where does it go? And what does that mean for our futures? For the people we pass history onto?

JOE RECOMMENDS

Rachael Allen's *Kingdomland* (Faber) was a big inspiration. I love how the poems oscillate an event, returning and returning to offer new and strange flashes. I also love Kim Hyesoon's *Autobiography of Death* (And Other Stories) for its playful approach to approximations of scale. Another book that helped me a lot was *Ghost of* by Diana Khoi Nguyen (Omnidawn Publishing). This, like *Kingdomland*, is an instance of a poet taking an event and then turning it over and over in their hand. White space is used in a really surprising way, and the poems had me rethinking my approach to narrative and autobiography.

the yellow summer of my childhood

Image: Joe Carrick-Varty

YOU WILL HAVE YOUR BODY SOON

all year   i visited a storm
the storm was ancient   the storm
like every storm   before it
was an iteration   of the first storm
it had rolled on   with its gusts
through many   violent afternoons
much clattering   in the trees
i was swimming   across a lake
my father a dot   on the shoreline
and the storm   was watching
or the storm was   inside my body
it's hard to say   we had come
to the lake as a treat   to make up
for an act of violence   and at some point
in all the excitement   i had swum too far
or i had swum   exactly far enough
my body   a pocket of weather
pushing out   across time
my body   high up somewhere
wanting the limit   of itself
O body   the things i will do
to make you   my own again
let's meet   in the middle
between violence   and the next
bout of   genuine happiness

Image: Rebecca Ribichini

WAYNE HOLLOWAY-SMITH

Wayne Holloway-Smith is the author of two poetry collections *Alarum* (2017) and *Love Minus Love* (Bloodaxe Books, 2020), which was shortlisted for the T.S. Eliot Prize and the Ledbury Munte Prize for Best Second Collection. He won The Poetry Society's Geoffrey Dearmer Prize in 2016 and The National Poetry Competition in 2018. He currently lives in London and is Editor of *The Poetry Review*.

RABBITBOX

SCRIBNER EDITIONS | £12.99 | PBS PRICE £9.75

RABBITBOX – a refuge, safe place and pressure cooker combined – riffs on repeated and telling "rabbit" terminology for fragility, fear and love. "Rabbit" is the pet name used by the mother for her son, "the boy with buck teeth", who is haunted, scared (and scarred) by ill-treatment. The two live together in the "rabbitbox" of fear, longing for escape from the despotism of the father. The "she" mother-figure placates the ever-present toxicity of the father-figure, with meals and conjugal rights (and rites). "She" embodies the struggle for survival in a destructive male domain. The child must be saved as the mother offers herself as sacrifice, or the mother saves herself and the child is sacrificed. This tug between the two generates the only true option of the collection – to find a way to save both mother and child.

Poetry breaks out as formally concentrated nuggets of feeling. Claustrophobia transmutes into moments of startling insight for the reader. There is a larger-than-life quality to the mother as saviour or betrayer. Her dignity is not negotiable, even when immersed by despotic male forces. The child, soft, open to affection, frightened, and observant, waits for his mother to do something about their joint terror. The offshoot is poetry with a bite of feeling and acutely observed instances of terror. In 'A Question' the narrator asks: "how much love does it take / to shrink a mother / away from her body / to the size of a little girl". Left and right justified texts and inch-sized blocks of language at the centre of the page evade conventional forms and show alternative modes of domesticity.

In 'Shadowgraphy' the poet constructs an imaginary that maps trauma by its frailties. "The theatre of the mind" is a recurring phrase that points to invention for survival and the serious play of the make-believe. 'A History' has many takes. "When She" takes decisive action and leaves the tyranny of the house "she left her body she left her adult body", suggesting an imagined separation or trauma reaction. 'A History' makes repeated revisits to the trauma, tending towards solace, if not cure. 'The Mother's Bedtime Story' allegorises the domestic to make a fearful situation bearable. 'A History' recurs as topic and poem, sometimes followed by a blank page of histories as yet unwritten, the breather that the reader needs to think, feel and read on. The collection takes its title and point of departure from Joseph Pintauro's *The Rabbit Box* (1970). Over to you, reader.

FRED D'AGUIAR

WAYNE HOLLOWAY-SMITH

Imagine a naïve lad, who failed at school and had not read a thing since, suddenly crouching in a dank alleyway, next to a line of bins, round the back of Portobello Road Market, to take in the pages of a book he's almost tripped over while not looking where he was going. It wouldn't be exaggerating to say this book has an almost magical effect on him. Layering image and text, moving through elliptical leaps of imagination and refrain, it engenders such an emotional register that this young lad doesn't quite know what to do with himself, or do next, apart from pocketing the book and taking it with him on his journey through the next twenty years.

The book is called *The Rabbit Box*, one in a series written by an ex-priest, poet and playwright called Joseph Pintauro and designed by Norman Laliberté. The naïve lad, you've probably guessed, is me on my first trip to West London, having arrived days before and begun to make my way in a big, intimidating city.

Through a series of wrong-turns, accidents, good and bad luck, I found myself two decades later, somehow, with two poetry collections under my belt, and owing a huge debt to that book. So, I began to write into, or through, some stylistic or tonal strategies of Pintauro's, as a means of paying homage. After a period, I felt, in a strange way, like I was being invited to depart from this ritual, to delve into the realm of my own unconscious, and begin creating, I think, a vocabulary through which I could express and ask some questions I'd been carrying for an even longer time than I'd been carrying Pintauro's *The Rabbit Box*.

Although what materialised bears little resemblance to my initial efforts, my new book would not exist without Pintauro's, or the beautiful coincidence of meeting it, that afternoon, so long ago.

WAYNE RECOMMENDS

Nuar Alsadir, *Animal Joy* (Fitzcarraldo Editions); Edwina Atlee, *a great shaking* (Tenement Press); Imogen Cassels, *Silk Work* (Prototype); Sasha Debevec-McKenney, *Joy Is My Middle Name* (Fitzcarraldo Editions); Byung-Chul Han, *The Crisis of Narration* (Polity); bonnie hancell + elle lowe, *a day at the beach the distance between us* (gong farm); Richard Scott, *That Broke into Shining Crystals* (Faber); Natalie Shapero, *Stay Dead* (Out-Spoken Press); Richard Siken, *I Do Know Some Things* (Chatto & Windus); Joelle Taylor, *Maryville* (Bloomsbury); Shrikant Verma, *Magadh* (And Other Stories).

Image: Jack Smyth

careful, careful – one slip, rabbit one bump
and suddenly the whole house is awake
and hymnal – a shadow's man-lunge
and *hosanna* the wallpaper is trumpeting
his hand, orchestral, his voice – *hosanna*
the pots some pans a shoe kicked
and the doorframe booms animate
something in him like a fist to the back
always hard blue veins
under dark blue jeans
a mother always
mute over the sink
at the edge of everything
no kind word but the place is ringing

Image: Adrian Pope

KEITH JARRETT

Keith Jarrett is a writer, performer, and educator from London. He is the author of the poetry collection *Selah* (Burning Eye Books, 2017), the play *Safest Spot in Town* (2017) and the poetry pamphlet *I Speak Home* (Eyewear, 2015). He has performed at and coordinated poetry festivals in English and Spanish in the UK and abroad. Jarrett is a former UK Poetry Slam Champion and won Rio de Janeiro's Literary Festival of the Urban Periphery (FLUPP) in 2014. His poetry show *Identity Mix-Up* (2013) premiered at the Edinburgh Festival Fringe. Jarrett teaches at NYU London, holds a PhD from Birkbeck College, and is a Lambda and Obsidian Fellow. He was selected for the International Literature Showcase.

HIDE ME UNDER THE BLOOD

BAD BETTY PRESS | £12.99 | PBS PRICE £9.75

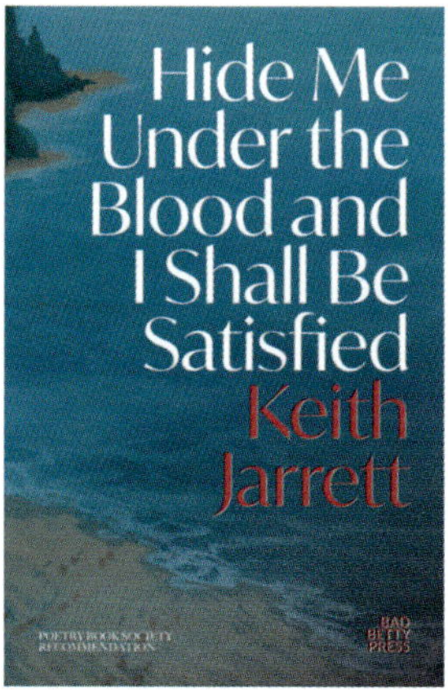

High church testimony and outrage powers these poems. They're elegiac too about the least expected of things (police brutality, poverty, low self-esteem) that coalesce into resolve and understanding. This emotional intelligence makes for the best poems that soar from a DJ's mix of rhetoric and rhythm in the prosody, and in the myriad ways that make a poem more than chopped up prose. Keith Jarrett's poetry elevates diction and syntax to that equation with feeling as meaning. You read and do not wish to argue with testimony. You feel and see what he's driving at, through the new avenues of experience opened up by these probing poems.

> what I hate about poetry is its abandon
> what I love about headlines is their brevities
> what I hate about the universe is its expansiveness
> what I love about love is its inheritance

His command of Spanish language and landscapes imbues an English language and island location with a double vision of feeling and meaning. He reconnects the island to the European mainland and historicises how we come to know our place in the poem and in our time. If his body is a way to heighten this sense of time and place, his reception as a Black male remains troubled. But out of that static of rejection and contradictory, but no less true, love of place, in the gaps and in-betweenness of the two, stands his work. If the poem is wiser than the poet (as the saying goes) then the reader is meant to be wiser than the poet by the poem's end. In the poem's afterlife (that time beyond the reading) it continues tunnelling into our senses and understanding of it. Surely, the reader helps Keith Jarrett through the impasse of race in a white space and maleness in a gesture towards twoness, if not a plural, gender.

> Tomorrow morning at the stroke of eleven – or queerabouts
> – all traces of heterosexuality will be eradicated.

This sounds more complicated than the matter-of-fact language of the poetry and the local delights of lines and imagery that suffuse the collection. There must be a way of saying that Keith Jarrett writes with an urgency and sense of emergency matched by the climate and politics, that his poetry intervenes memorably in some of the most pressing debates of our times.

FRED D'AGUIAR

KEITH JARRETT

"If we must die, let it not be like hogs" begins Claude McKay's sonnet from 1919 that would come to symbolise the Harlem Renaissance, the defiance of his words striking despite – or perhaps due to – its conventional form. Decades later, in his essay 'History of the Voice', Kamau Brathwaite insists "the hurricane doesn't roar in pentameter", rejecting the sonnet and the rigid metric of colonial standard English.

McKay, Brathwaite, and other "patron saints" I adopted for this collection – including Audre Lorde, Edwin Morgan, and Camille Claudel (Rodin's spurned lover) – have become my grapple partners in excavating form, language, sound, and the violence of cultural and religious heritage. While *Hide Me Under the Blood and I Shall Be Satisfied* is not a polemic per se, each poem is a dialogue, a reasoning, punctuated by mischief.

My 'wind sucked between teeth' sequence, which serves as a playful gear change in between poems, came from discovering a 2015 article in a French newspaper, 'Mais c'est quoi, le tchip?', discussing the ban on pupils kissing their teeth in classrooms. For the uninitiated, it's an expression of anger or frustration among many African diaspora cultures, one that only requires "spit and tongue".

Subversion of language is a rich territory I always draw from, along with music and song, from hymns to Soca lyrics, from Calypso as Windrush "origin story" to the Reggaetón of Daddy Yankee as a nostalgia machine. The titular poem 'Hide Me Under the Blood, Lord' takes inspiration from a church song I remember from my youth, but I give it darker undertones as "my blood cries out" from the "Cains of my uncles". Here, and elsewhere, violent biblical references prevail.

McKay re-emerges in my final poem 'Inland', as I make peace with the sonnet and with religious inheritance, inverting his lines to forge new understandings.

KEITH RECOMMENDS

Sanah Ahsan, *I cannot be good until you say it* (Bloomsbury); Billy-Ray Belcourt, *The Idea of an Entire Life* (Carcanet); Julia Bell, *Hymnal* (Parthian); Caroline Bird, *The Air Year* (Carcanet); Leo Boix ed., *Hemisferio Cuir* (Fourteen Poems); Desree, *Altar* (Bad Betty); Gustav Parker Hibbett, *High Jump As Icarus Story* (Banshee); Michael Mullen, *Goonie* (Corsair); Gboyega Odubanjo, *Adam* (Faber); Carl Phillips, *Scattered Snows, To the North* (Carcanet); Danez Smith, *Bluff* (Chatto & Windus); Joelle Taylor, *Maryville* (Bloomsbury); Pádraig Ó Tuama, *Kitchen Hymns* (Cheerio).

Sugar is thicker than blood. Watch me dis s o l v e.

Image: Kerry Ticlo

SKANK

V. [T]

London is the place, he sings
into the history books of
Blackness in these Isles;
a Calypsonian faux free—
styling his way into
the blessed Motherland.
After, reels of *Blues dance*:
black and white couples,
backs bent, elbows raised.
Establishment looks askance
at syncopated movement,
jerking like the spirit's taken.
Glance through three score
and ten years since; our
reframing carries in the knees.
And we can't seem to step past
this sinking shipwreck tale, still
framing us off-beat; beaten;
swept in on a broken wave.

Image: Tereza Červeňová

JENNIFER WONG

Jennifer Wong is a Hong Kong-born poet who lives in the UK. She studied English at Oxford and has an MA and PhD in creative writing from University of East Anglia and Oxford Brookes. She has published three collections including *Letters Home* (Nine Arches Press) and is the co-editor of *State of Play: Poets of East and Southeast Asian Heritage in Conversation* (Out-spoken Press, 2023) and *Where Else: An International Hong Kong Poetry Anthology* (Verve, 2023). She is also the author of *Identity, Home and Writing Elsewhere* (Bloomsbury, 2023). She is currently editing *Woman, Mapped*, a Rebecca Swift Foundation women's poetry anthology forthcoming from Fly on the Wall Press in 2026.

LIGHT YEAR

NINE ARCHES PRESS | £11.99 | PBS PRICE £9.00

Light Year follows Jennifer Wong's 2020 *Letters Home* 回家 and, like this earlier collection, these vivid, delicate, and multifaceted poems unpick the intricacies of existing between nations, languages, and cultures. The collection opens with two epigraphs, the second of which is from Elizabeth Bishop's 1952 poem 'Arrival at Santos' that ends with the line, "we are driving to the interior". While this clearly describes a journey from the city of Santos, Brazil, a shift from the port city to a more remote location, it is also a metaphor for a journey of deeper self-discovery, reflecting Bishop's own experiences of displacement and feeling "at home". This internal anxiety of belonging is reflected in Wong's remarkable work, particularly in 'Softest Memory', 'Time Difference' and 'Because' – made even more impactful and devastating through the echo of its profound refrain:

because I wasn't born here   my hair comes out the wrong colour
because I wasn't born here   I've grown up loving Satsuke's magic Totoro instead

Light Year is divided into four sections, each delving into the mind of a poet crossing spaces of deep wounds, love, and healing, creating a constellation of friendships and devotion as the poems deftly chart her progress through upheaval and change. In 'Twelve Questions' the speaker explains, "I am a beginner and am always beginning". Wong brings a clarity and lightness to intensely complex ideas of time, space, memory, and legacy, as well as to tricky and intangible states like dissatisfaction, alienation, loneliness and insecurity – and with wonderfully sharp humour too, as in 'AIBU':

For my birthday I'd like
to ask DH for a weekend getaway:
a hotel room with a nespresso machine

Wong draws the reader into a tender confidence, at once revealing and particular, so that reading *Light Year* is a remarkably intimate and almost conspiratorial experience. The collection offers glimpses into the journeys of a migrant and a mother, at what it is we hold dear in life, and the tension inherent in the time difference between memories and place. These are intelligent and beautifully philosophical poems that skilfully navigate the expectations and beliefs which shape, confine, trouble, and liberate us, "But the poem assembles itself in the air, and a few deep / thinkers move through a deep space without stairs".

VICTORIA KENNEFICK

JENNIFER WONG

To me, writing *Light Year* feels very different from *Letters Home*, my earlier Nine Arches Press collection. When I worked on *Letters Home*, I was on solid, safer ground, reflecting on my journeys as a (younger) migrant. When it comes to *Light Year*, I relied on instinct and feeling. In the light year(s), there is so much change and, in the middle of it all, the pain of silence, the struggle with queer feelings, and of thinking and living impossibly as a mother and a woman writer.

A lot of my poems emerge from scribblings and phone notes during my work journeys (bus journeys in Guildford, tube journeys, or the weekly train commutes to Oxford and some metro journeys in Hong Kong from the last time I went). Some were born in the early hours of the morning when I was an insomniac, and pained by the precarity of this AI-driven world we live in. Some of the poems correspond to recent lived experiences and memories of friendships and love I held onto. Relationships that haven't worked out (including marriage), and how I feel about myself and others I care about. What we need in this world to stay true to ourselves and how we give permission to let our poems correspond with what we don't fully understand.

Some of the poems were born because I couldn't find a way to reconcile the different facets of myself, particularly the strangeness of being a mother, migrant and writer. In the process, I started from not knowing what I wanted to say, to realising that I have to trust the poem's evolving nature. Reading or rereading other poets' work, especially women poets' writings helped me to grapple with silences and grief, the intersections and the fluidity of longing and identity.

I hope that those who read these poems can gain a glimpse of me, my private world and my imagination. More than that, I hope these poems can offer courage for women (mothers, not-mothers) to claim the space they deserve and let poetry into their lives.

JENNIFER RECOMMENDS

Romalyn Ante, *AGIMAT* (Chatto & Windus); Mona Arshi, *Mouth* (Penguin); Leo Boix, *Southernmost Sonnets* (Chatto & Windus); Maya Caspari, *Almost, with Tenderness* (Out-spoken); Niall Campbell, *The Island in the Sounds* (Bloodaxe Books); *The Poems of Seamus Heaney* (Faber); Sarah Howe, *Foretokens* (Chatto & Windus); Theresa Muñoz, *Archivum* (Pavilion); Richard Siken, *I Do Know Some Things* (Chatto & Windus); Arthur Sze, *Into the Hush* (Penguin); Jessica Traynor, *New Arcadia* (Bloodaxe); Anon, *Poetry Is Not Luxury* (Galley UK).

And in the room we could hear
the ocean waves, breaking against
The history of ourselves.

Image: Sandy Litchfield

TWELVE QUESTIONS

After Bhanu Kapil

I am allergic to silence. I fill a silent room with my nonsensical humming.

I am a beginner and am always beginning. Every beginning is different and so daunting. I begin with the simplest wants, to make something that hasn't been before.

I now live in the middle of an iridescent lake. Here I could feel nothing but water. The water is very real and all that I could touch for now. Water so pure and icy cold and shapeless. Water shifting around me.

I am in love with hope itself: radical hope that grows like wild grass.

I came from a city so safe we had problems imagining anything at all happening. A city of subways and footbridges and train doors opening and closing.

Whenever I pass by a tree stump I am reminded of dismembered bodies, dismembered memories, disconnected friends.

My body is imperfect. Marked with history, my body feels like so many opaque, turquoise glass pieces polished by the sea.

I dreamt that I woke up without fear, convinced that the duel had finally ended. When I woke up from the dream I knew it hadn't.

I am responsible for my mother's suffering.

What's left to say or explain if we ever meet again?

How will you prepare for your death?

The earth is full of memories. Before the atrocity.
This is the earth that I'll kiss at the end.

Image: Andrew Downes

RITA ANN HIGGINS

Rita Ann Higgins was born in 1955 in Galway, where she still lives. She left school at fourteen, and was in her late twenties when she started writing poetry. She has since published many books of poetry and prose, including *Sunny Side Plucked* (Poetry Book Society Recommendation, 1996), *An Awful Racket* (2001), *Throw in the Vowels: New & Selected Poems* (2005), *Ireland Is Changing Mother* (2011) and *Tongulish* (2016) from Bloodaxe; *Hurting God: Prose & Poems* (2010), *Our Killer City: isms, chisms, chasms and chisms: essays and poems* (2018) and *Pathogens Love a Patsy: Pandemic & Other Poems* (2020) from Salmon; and *The Long Weekend* (Gill, 2024) Her 2026 Bloodaxe retrospective, *Jiving with Wasps: New & Selected Poems*, draws on all these collections as well as later work. Her appearances on the Brendan O'Connor Show during and since the pandemic earned her even wider popularity in Ireland – reading her poems to audiences of over 400,000 on the weekend shows – with O'Connor calling her "the people's poet". She is a member of Aosdána.

JIVING WITH WASPS

BLOODAXE BOOKS | £14.99 | PBS PRICE £11.25

If you call Rita Ann Higgins a National Treasure to her face you might risk, at a minimum, a tongue-lashing, and more than likely, a cuff or a slap. At least that's my lasting impression from her feisty poetry. Not that you'd think so when you meet her as I did way back in the early 90s at Cúirt, where she read and brought down the house with laughs and applause. She's sweet in person; but pugnacious, stalwart, eye-opening, in her imaginary offerings. Celebration of the everyday, that we may take for granted, powers much of these poems that span some forty years.

Women come across as prophets of routine. They suffer the ways of men in their lives with a faith that time will transform those men into decent folk by their proximity to women or by sheer will power. In a significant number of poems, the task of reforming men appears unwieldy, like trying to turn an oil tanker. It takes miles of patience to see the results, if any can be discerned. Her women are self-sufficient, patient, idealistic, and recondite. Rita Ann Higgins's poetry uplifts the spirit, through Covid, political upheaval and domestic despair.

In 'Goddess on the Mervue Bus' myth and fable-like tones make the quotidian heraldic, visionary. A nascent feminist spirit haunts lines replete with humour. There is a standup comedic element to some of the generous helpings of this selection. If men sometimes take on monstrous shapes and mannerisms, women can thwart their own liberation with acts of complicity and placation.

O Goddess on the Mervue bus,
no scrap dealer fashioned
you from memory or want,
you were spun from golden
dust, a dash of dream.

The Catholic church stands in the dock of conscience and conscientiousness underpinning Rita Ann Higgins's oeuvre. She forgives but you won't forget how she shapes her acts of absolution in her poetry. The town and country, nay the whole island, shines in her tones of light and dark with the occasional blast of colour. Long may she reign, at least unofficially, as Irish Poet Laureate.

FRED D'AGUIAR

THE BEES ARE COMING

Didn't we miss
lots of seasons that time.
Wasn't it mostly dark and darker?
The sameness of things was hard to stomach.

Snowdrops, daffodils and crocuses
gave us colder days,
but we loved their coats and colours.

Now you notice the morning light
getting earlier and earlier.
The birdsong is welcome,
you nearly hold your breath to listen,
you never knew nature
and the seasons meant so much.

The buds are peeping
and popping.
Cherry blossom with its pink gush and blush
is ahead of you on all journeys –
pick-ups and drop-offs
walks to the local beach.

The tadpoles are busy.
The caterpillar move is slow
but it is on,
entire families of them.

The bees are coming
looking for nectar.
We are nicer
looking for nectar too.
We are smiling –
hope is hanging around
seedlings are sprouting
spring is here.

CHEN YUHONG

DIANA SHI & GEORGE O'CONNELL

Chen Yuhong was born in Kaohsiung, Taiwan, and graduated from the Wenzao Ursuline University of Languages. After a decade in Canada, she returned to Taiwan. The editors of the annual *Best Poetry of Taiwan* named her Poet of the Year for her 2004 collection *Annotations*. Her collection *Bewitched* (2007) received Taiwan's Chinese Writers & Artists Association's Poetry Award. Her most recent poetry collection *Half-light* was awarded the International Cikada Prize in poetry.

George O'Connell, editor and translator with Diana Shi, has received numerous honours for his own poetry, including *Atlanta Review*'s International Grand Prize and the Pablo Neruda Award, two US National Endowment for the Arts Literature Translation Fellowships. He served as Fulbright Professor to Peking University and National Taiwan University.

Diana Shi is a co-recipient of two US National Endowment for the Arts Literature Translation Fellowships. Shi has collaborated since 2006 with George O'Connell in translating many prominent Chinese-speaking poets. In 2012 they launched *Pangolin House*, an international journal of poetry and art (www.pangolinhouse.com).

IMPOSSIBLE PARADISE

TRANSLATED BY GEORGE O'CONNELL & DIANA SHI

CARCANET PRESS | £14.99 | PBS PRICE £11.25

Impossible Paradise 不可能的天堂, *Selected Poems* by Taiwanese poet Chen Yuhong, is a world both meticulously observed and gloriously uncontainable. It is a book of looking, through microscope and telescope alike, translated with luminous tact and precision by Diana Shi and George O'Connell. Chen's poems, originally written in Mandarin, roam from Che Guevara to Rubén Darío, from the sheen of falling snow to the ghostly serenade of Chopin's *Opus 35*, from the fragile petal of a cherry blossom to the obliterated Buddhas of Bamiyan.

> Buddha lives amid rubble, amid the broken,
> amid the colossal task.

Through the translators' attentiveness, what could have been an atlas of disparate wonders becomes a continuous hum of intelligence and tenderness. Shi and O'Connell have rendered not only Chen's meanings but her manner of seeing – that quicksilver movement between the minute and the cosmic, the human and the historical. The translation listens acutely to Chen's cadences: the "pulsating rhythm" of her poetics, her habit of finding eternity in a cat's stare or a drifting cloud.

In 'Here', a cat's "ice-blue eyes" mirror "unknown birds aloft, / the wind, and us"– an image that feels as crisp in English as it must in Mandarin. At its best, the English feels more like transference than translation – a migration of sensibility. In 'White Moth Orchid' the poet notes:

> How life can pass
> beheld at sunset's window
> the moment it leaves the stem,
> the sound a faint
> *gatha* of one word, tidy and final.

The translators make that finality sing, precise yet unforced. *Impossible Paradise* is a triumph of shared seeing: Chen's expansive curiosity is refracted through two English voices attuned to her every shimmer. It generously invites us to dwell in the impossible – made vividly possible through translation.

LEO BOIX

CHERRY BLOSSOM SONNET

This pink-skirted gypsy girl, this laughter in surprise,
this cloud of dazzling hair,
these petals adrift through Kyoto's April
in raucous philosophy.
This blue sky, this river, this flowering moment.
This life all too brief—speak not
of eternity. This sunlight
not light but a flood of gametes, male and female,
this flowering no flower but desire.
Soaring moments of flame, unreal disorderly beauty of loss, loss.
These footprints deep or shallow, entranced
at April being April. These blooms, this ripe
body's spirit swelling from innocence
to be lost
in a riot of cherry blossoms,
this Ecclesiastes of spring, this memorandum
of life and death the hourglass' inverted emptiness.
This tray of spring the silence of dust and ash.

Image: Peter Tindborg

FATEMA ABDOOLCARIM

Fatema Abdoolcarim is an Indian-Pakistani Hong Konger who makes films and writes. Her films have been shown internationally, including at Locarno Film Festival, Montreal Museum of Fine Arts, and Osaka Asian Film Festival. *Tremble* is her debut collection of poetry. She lives in the Baltic Sea, on the island of Bornholm.

TREMBLE

MONITOR BOOKS | £12.00 |

In this strikingly assured and searing pamphlet, Fatema Abdoolcarim writes the intimate on bodily parchments and, in so doing, she traces the pain that a woman's body has to endure and live in the name of fertility and motherhood. The poet pushes against vulnerability and dwells on the very meaning of a woman's body, not as a body in isolation, but as a body in relation. What we see within the folds of these poems are rewritings of/as journeys, whereby "trembling", both corporeally and figuratively, is a rhythmic recalibration of the body at work. The final poem 'Tremor' forms an etymological bond with the title of the book, a common pulse, as if this "trembling" is the body itself and with every movement something first-hand is created:

> the back of my hand, bony like bird feet
> trembling, the barn owl floats close
> if I reach out I could touch the tip of his wing.

Through destruction, albeit self-inflicted, Abdoolcarim forges a new body from scattered individual pieces, re-assembling the "shards" of her previous self. Tacitly and contrary to the loud "smashing" that happens before our eyes, the poet reasserts a body of her own making and, in the process, creates an/other whose own assemblage is a combination of the poet's blood, past and present:

> The bowl is now in thirty-six pieces.
> She gathers each shard, each flake, wipes them clean, fits them
> together, takes out the gold. With this blood men are made.

Like the umbilical cord that attaches the mother and the child, eventually to be severed to sustain them both, Abdoolcarim actively engages the skin, or what she astutely calls "skinship", to shed light on the intergenerational body – how bodies touch, but also mark and bruise each other in the process.

> I was never held skin to skin by my grandmother.
> Though in old age I held her body, rippled with soft bones,
> steady in the bathroom.

In *Tremble*, the body is a coming testimony to what is taking place inside us but also in the open, in this callous world. To borrow Natalie Diaz's words from another setting, the poems in our hands are precisely about "(a)utonomous lives in collective living", where the intimate and the global are one.

YOUSIF M. QASMIYEH & ALYCIA PIRMOHAMED

TREMOR

I hear him before I see him.
An underbelly of bright white light
a ghost in the shadows.

With pitch black eyes
he sees into pitch blackness.
Swooping softly in figure ∞'s—

immensity held open in his wings
held almost entirely still
except for a slight tremble

unseen, but felt by my fingertips.
It quivers up my arms into my chest
makes my heart beat

and he feels it too—
the back of my hand, bony like bird feet
trembling, the barn owl floats close

if I reach out I could touch the tip of his wing.

SPRING BOOK REVIEWS

HARRY BAKER: TENDER

REVIEWED BY DAVE COATES

Tender is a very gentle concept album, a dad's-eye account of new parenthood. The poems are charming, gentle, whimsical or rhapsodic, and, though peppered with doctors' appointments and anxiety attacks, the book's goal is, primarily, to encourage and console new parents in turn. Its shortcomings are primarily formal: 100 poems is too many, and a more satisfying (if less marketable) book might have trimmed some samey pieces. Still, *Tender* is playful and engaging, a curious and thoughtful account.

CANONGATE | £14.99 (HB) | PBS PRICE £11.25

RISHI DASTIDAR: CHERRY BLOSSOM AT NIGHTBREAK

REVIEWED BY DAVE COATES

You go out on a limb because that's where the fruit is. Rishi Dastidar has always swung for the fences in his poems of romantic yearning and satisfaction alike, and, though *Cherry Blossom at Nightbreak* hits more often than not, even the whiffs are charming, animated as they are by the poet's abiding loves: the verbose and the grandiose. The final poem is an understated toast, blessing the reader into the cherry-tinted night. Dastidar's oeuvre remains curious and playful, each book an evolution.

NINE ARCHES PRESS | £11.99 | PBS PRICE £9.00

RUPINDER KAUR WARAICH: TIGRESS WITH WINGS

REVIEWED BY SHASH TREVETT

A coming-of-age collection which seeks to decipher what it is to be a woman. Rich in the Panjabi language and folktales, Waraich's poems muse on finding love, losing it, yearning for it. Placing herself among other women (her mother, Panjabi artists, writers and actresses from Bollywood) Waraich examines how women actualise themselves as "the orange and red" of flames. Lingering, like the refrains of a ghazal, are lovers from Panjabi folktales who help dissect the chasm between childhood and adulthood, fairy tale and reality.

SEREN BOOKS | £10.99 | PBS PRICE £8.25

THE WRITING SQUAD

SIMON MADDRELL: LAMPING WILD RABBITS

REVIEWED BY JASMINE GRAY

In Simon Maddrell's arresting debut collection threat and desire live side-by-side. Each poem is a glare against the sea, guiding us through the rocky shores of reclamation in the face of erasure. Declaring "it is language that restores our place", Maddrell's ghosts of siblings, lovers and languages haunt every line, startling and unashamed. These are poems of endurance, of looking forward to a new world, dragging our feet in the dirt as we go.

OUT-SPOKEN PRESS | £11.99 | PBS PRICE £9.00

JOHN McCULLOUGH: CROWD VOLTAGE

REVIEWED BY JENNY DANES

Crowd Voltage is a lively, striking exploration of community and connectedness. McCullough paints the body as part of something bigger, whether celestial, architectural, or ecological – these poems examine class, queer lineage, and our "non-human family". Piers, internal organs, and animals recur throughout the book, and we are treated to delightful images: a magpie wears "a stained black and white tracksuit", popcorn kernels leap "like tiny goats / who had only just discovered how to jump". A bright and thoughtful book.

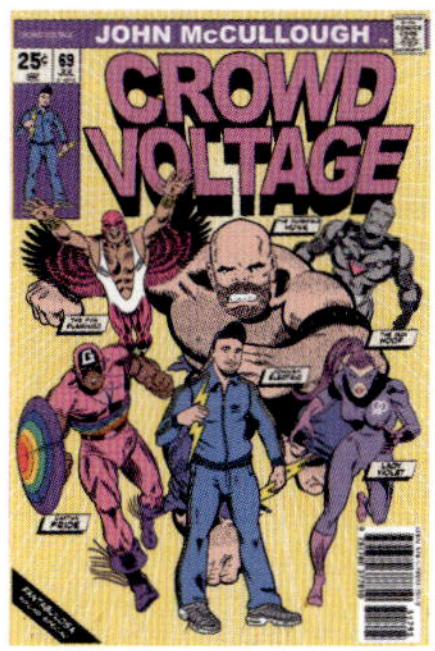

BLOODAXE BOOKS | £12.99 | PBS PRICE £9.75

RAQUEL F. MENÉNDEZ: THE POSTHUMOUS BOOK OF SHAHRAZAD

REVIEWED KAYLEIGH JAYSHREE

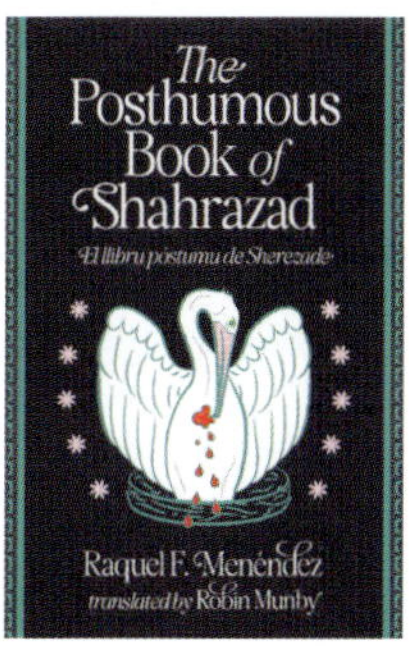

"Desire, desire with which we transform what we love" goes the final line in a section of *The Posthumous Book of Shahrazad* by Raquel F. Menéndez, translated by Robin Munby. Throughout the collection, fragments of identity, belonging and the speaker's sense create tension. The verses are scattered in flight, in tension and in conversation with the original poems in the second half of the book. The collection plays with the familiar and colloquial, said and unsaid.

SKEIN PRESS | £11.00 | PBS PRICE £9.00

SEAN O'BRIEN: THE BONFIRE PARTY

REVIEWED BY DAVE COATES

It's an odd decision to title this book after a painting that invokes 1933, and to heavily foreground Orwell's concerns about British complacency regarding fascism, when the poems themselves are barely concerned with either. It's deeply distracting to read O'Brien's allusive, ironic lyrics, waiting in vain for them to deliver on the book's framing. Nonetheless, *The Bonfire Party* retains O'Brien's usual high standard in its delicate music, near-effortless lyrical flow and obsession with Heaney-ish stallings and suspensions of grammar and time.

PICADOR | £10.99 | PBS PRICE £8.25

MEGAN PATTIE: BERTHA COMES DOWN

REVIEWED BY DAVE COATES

Pattie's debut collection dives deep into the places where nature and imagination meet, their shared dark and fungal corners. Partly a book of spells – that is, statements of wish and will – and partly an entomologist's-eye view of woods, caves, mushrooms and myths, the collection's great strengths are in applying fairy-tale beats and motifs to the brute realities of nature and the human psyche. *Bertha Comes Down* is an assured, painterly first collection.

BROKEN SLEEP BOOKS | £12.99 | PBS PRICE £9.75

CATHERINE REDFORD: THE WAY THE WATER HELD ME

REVIEWED BY BETH DAVIES

In this "collage of grief" the speaker's mourning for her wife is refracted through lenses from the historical and literary to the raw and dreamlike. Skies, oceans, ABBA songs, and bedsheets are all "somehow emitting her absence". The speaker becomes "animal smell / dirt-coated claws", or a ruin with "walls unbuilt by winters". But the book's heart is in conversations with novelist Mary Shelley, also mourning her spouse. Through shipwrecks, séances, and found poetry, Redford and Shelley "survey the aftermath" of widowhood together.

THE EMMA PRESS | £10.99 | PBS PRICE £8.25